BEFORE READING THE BOOK PLEASE READ THIS DISCLAIMER

The information presented in this book is educational in nature and is provided only as general information. As part of the information contained in this book, you understand you will be introduced to using a pendulum (an intuitive communication device) and provided information about various charts which can be used with a pendulum. By reading this book you understand the author and publisher do not know how you will personally respond to using a pendulum and whether your use of a pendulum and/or any of the charts will help you with a particular issue. You agree to assume and accept full responsibility for any and all risks associated with reading this book and using a pendulum and/or any of the charts contained in this book.

The information contained in this book is not intended to represent that the use of a pendulum and/or any of the charts are used to diagnose, treat, cure, or prevent any disease or psychological disorder. The use of a pendulum and/or any of the charts is not a substitute for medical or psychological treatment. Consequently, reading the book and using a pendulum and/or any of the charts for yourself does not replace health care from medical/psychological professionals. You agree to consult with your health care provider for any specific medical/psychological problems. In addition, you understand that any information contained in the book is not to be considered a recommendation that you stop seeing any of your health care professionals or using prescribed medication, if any, without consulting with your health care professional, even if after reading the book and using a pendulum and/or any of the charts it appears and indicates that such medication or therapy is unnecessary.

The author and publisher accept no responsibility or liability whatsoever for the use or misuse of the information contained in this book. The author strongly advises that you seek professional advice as appropriate before implementing any protocol or opinion expressed in this book, including using a pendulum and/or any of the charts, and before making any health decision.

By continuing to read this book, you knowingly, voluntarily, and intelligently assume these risks, including any adverse outcome that might result from using a pendulum and/or any of the charts, and agree to release, indemnify, hold harmless and defend the author and publisher, and their respective heirs, agents, consultants, and employees from and against any and all claims which you, or your heirs and/or representatives, may have for any loss, damage, or injury of any kind or nature arising out of or in connection with reading this book and using a pendulum and/or any of the charts. If any court of law rules that any part of this Disclaimer is invalid, the Disclaimer stands as if those parts were struck out.

BY CONTINUING TO READ THE BOOK YOU AGREE TO THIS DISCLAIMER

Radiesthesia II
Vital Force in the human body

© 2019 Christopher Freeland. All rights reserved. Any unauthorized use of this publication is prohibited by law. No part of this publication may be reproduced or transmitted in any form or by any means, electronic or mechanical, including photocopying, recording, or any information storage and retrieval system for public and/or private use without permission in writing from the publisher.

ISBN:

Radiesthesia II

Vital Force in the human body

CONTENTS

INTRODUCTION

OVERVIEW

BRIEF HISTORY OF RADIESTHESIA

VITAL FORCE

COLOURS

SPIRIT RELEASE

THE THUMBKEY

FACTORS IN ANALYSIS

WITNESS

DIAGNOSIS/ANALYSIS

THE MAGNETIC COMPONENT

TW2 – PRESENCE OF GEOPATHIC STRESS (GS)

RESISTANCE

GENERAL STATE

NERVOUS STATE

EMOTIONAL STATE

MENTAL STATE

VITAL FORCE

HUN & PO

MAGNETISM

ELECTRIC CURRENT

ABOUT THE AUTHOR

INTRODUCTION

It seems that a method to navigate between the dimensions of spirit and material reality would be most welcome. Whether it is a bridge to find a sense to the human experience of waking, dreaming and sleep; the physical and invisible spirit worlds; the cosmic and terrestrial. A bridge that restores communications which we have managed to lose, for whatever reasons. An access to truth and harmony. The idea being to enable a greater degree of self-sufficiency.

For some, it could be astrology; for others, divining in some form or other. For me, it is radiesthesia.

Access to the truth, however trivial, however relative, can only be of benefit. The trick is determining how relative and that requires a firm understanding of what you are doing, of what is happening, and most importantly, if possible, a perfect balance in the role of the bridge.

In the final analysis, you are 'doing' nothing, you are merely open to the space where you are, you do not even have a choice in the matter, you are. You can allow the ego to chip in, but that is probably the extent of your true free will. So, do away with any notion of action, authorship, ownership, it can only get you into trouble and the false belief that you are some kind of cause/effect, or channel in whatever is going on, therefore distracting you from the task at hand.

A closer look at what might be going on

For ease of understanding, I will start with the currently accepted notion that it is the brain which deals with thinking. Further on in our studies, we will take a look at the traditional Chinese attitude towards organ function, and the brain is not an organ in their system. It is of interest and quite revealing that a relatively modern western theory partially corroborates that it is the small intestine which plays a major part in this thinking process, rather than some zone of the brain.

The cerebral conscious element, the "mind" or intellect, is a powerful tool but with severe limitations because it functions in close collaboration with the emotions, those sensations acquired by means of individual experience and our education (parents, teachers, books, movies, music, etc.). This "mind" has nothing whatsoever to do with reality, it is a constant chimera of images, subject to personal interpretation, nevertheless sometimes shared with others, when we call it the world. There seems little point developing further the numerous ideas that abound around this subject. It has been done by others far more qualified and competent than I.

So much for the individual human component, but what about the cyclical world of Nature? The world of the waking state? That is what this booklet investigates in its modest way. It is, however, based on a very firm conviction, which goes as follows:

The real stuff of existence-consciousness (spirit) is universal, and that word contains a clue, uni, or the oneness that is the canvas on which all our feelings and perceptions can find expression. This is what I call the **all-conscious**. It is always there, nothing can affect it, everything has it and nothing can be without it.

By using a pendulum one is simply calling out to this all-conscious because that is where everything is deposited, including knowledge. This depository is not to be found in any of the so-called faculties of the conscious cerebral mind, or in the cells which are constantly dying and being replaced.

Call it what you will, it is not bothered by names. IT IS.

OVERVIEW

There is nothing magic about radiesthesia, unless you believe that the world is magic in which case I agree totally!

Assuming that life is a vibrant whole and we are a small part of that totality, there comes a time when to know or to intuit something becomes an integral part of the knowledge, with a blending of subject-object and a momentary disappearance of individuality. That is the ideal state to be achieved if one is to be successful no matter what the form of practice used to discover the truth.

Of the various and surprising methods for finding out if something is good or bad for you, true or false, there are: the Bi-Digital O Ring Test (BIDORT), the friction test (with thumb and forefinger nail), the sway test, the toe-touching test, the arm test. These are all very efficient but not nearly as convenient or practical as the pendulum which requires only one person, allows the use of charts with the advantage of being discrete and can be done almost anywhere.

For practical reasons, I shall concentrate on the actual handling of a pendulum rather than the Y- or L-rods. The mental preparation and process is similar for all of them.

The secret of dowsing lies in thought and its expression. Generally, this thought comes into your mind as a question because you are not sure of something and want an answer, as in what is right or wrong, good or bad for you or the person for whom you are working. If the question is carefully formulated and you calmly allow it the time to circulate in the space where thoughts hang out, the reaction to the question – yes or no – impacts the nerves and causes muscular movement, providing the answer.

It is essential to avoid any ambiguity, so exercises to form clear, precise formulation are more than welcome, as we saw in the first part of this series. Equally important is the fact that radiesthesia is a binary affair.

One can only obtain a "yes" or "no" answer, no matter what the method used, so the way of seeking information needs to be adapted to that binary possibility. It takes practice and adapted methodology, but like so many other aspects of life, one learns and finds solutions.

Intense training and practice is necessary if you are to acquire a certain confidence. That does not mean that mistakes will not be made but when they are, the practice will have formed a data base in which you will be able to discover what it was that went wrong. Almost inevitably it is due to not respecting one or a number of the self-imposed criteria. It is a very self-disciplined affair, the mistakes are yours, so accept that responsibility and humility will lessen the bitterness!

More than in any other domain, one learns from one's mistakes. That may be painful but it's not the end of the world, whereas not learning brings the end of the world on faster!

A pendulum can be made of any solid material (wood, stone, metal, crystal) weighing from a few to several tens of grams, the form has no importance so long as it suspended on a string or thread which is held between the thumb and forefinger with the palm of the hand facing downwards and a relaxed wrist. You can use almost anything to obtain an answer, a piece of string with a ring or even a metal nut attached, a blade of grass if it can move with sufficient flexibility.

Personally, the pendulum is my tool of predilection, mainly because you only need one hand to use it and in conjunction with a chart, the questioning process and time is substantially reduced thus avoiding fatigue and potential mistakes. However, the choice of pendulum or rods is a very subjective affair, and very much depends on what your use is.

BRIEF HISTORY OF RADIESTHESIA

The term radiesthesia (the perception of waves/radiation) was coined by Abbé Boulay, a French Catholic priest in 1920 or so. There are a number of epithets employed for the same discipline: dowsing, divining, geomancy, water-witching, but as you can see, they are more restrictive than this neat expression.

It has been going on for a long time, perhaps even in prehistoric times, for there seems to be evidence from cave drawings that man's relationship with animals had something to do with a psychic location mechanism. It is of course hard to prove this, let alone the Sumerian, Egyptian or Babylonian applications, and it is of little importance because you can always ask the pendulum if this was the case!

It is a little known fact that mineral exploration companies throughout the world rely on people rather than machines to prospect for resources underground. Common or garden people with a pendulum or dowsing rods in hand can make or break the world's major corporations!

In more recent recorded history, radiesthesia has been going on for a long time, Louis XIV employed Martine de Bertereau to find precious minerals, he ended up throwing her in jail as he did not want to pay her and her husband, but that was not because of her capacities, I would hasten to add! The US Marines trained some of their personnel in the use of dowsing to detect mines and tunnels during the Vietnam war. As an anecdote, I trained quite a number of my Cambodian Buddhist student monks in Chiang Mai to use the pendulum, especially to search for unexploded ordinance once they returned home.

Abbé Mermet, a French priest and inventor of the pendulum that goes by his name, found numerous mineral deposits in South America for mining companies from his desk in France in the 1920s and 30s.

Radiesthesia can be performed locally or remotely, perhaps because it is not dependent on the time-space notion which governs our rational mindset. The bottom line is that it works, but receives little attention because it cannot be explained by scientific reasoning. As stated elsewhere, Radiesthesia holds no truck with empiricism (experience based on observation of the five or however many senses we have), we are in the domain of mentation, the space where everything starts and finishes. Anyone who tells you otherwise is not only ignorant but doing radiesthesia a dis-service.

There is no need to attribute irrelevant extraneous factors to it, whether physical or magical. There is no reason to claim scientific approval for what we are doing, science can have no place in this realm. There is nothing magical about this either, so you can have a totally clear conscience and forget about all the new-age nonsense one hears.

Quite a number of books have been written on this subject, but none to my knowledge deal with the critical subject of how dowsing actually works.

There is a permanent ongoing relationship operating in Nature which we profit from but never question, because it just happens and we are very unlikely to work out how it functions because we are part of it! The energy or life force ensures, among its many functions, communication between all the components making up our world. Were it not the case there could be no continuity, let alone that remarkable sensation we have of everything being in its place.

The cerebral conscious function of the brain, or whatever bit it is which asks the questions, being limited to the material phenomenal world of the physical senses, asks questions of the entity which has access to the answers, namely the aether-space where everything that has taken place in the past, now or will take place in the future. That entity is in communion with all dimensions – physical, emotional, mental and spiritual in the human, and the myriad forms for other beings; all of which share a "trace" of the life force involved. That entity-space can be accessed by means of a special form of applied thought, which one uses when dowsing.

In actual fact, the thought form is not so special. We all have it, we all know and experience it – at least at some stage in our lives, but few develop it.

The key to success in finding answers to questions is clear, specific, concentrated thought. That directs the question in hand and establishes the connection of that thought, without any parasitic influence, to the object which is no different from the thought itself, inasmuch as it shares the same aether-space.

_____

As you are probably aware, there were two schools of radiesthesia. What I advocate falls into neither school. The majority of French authors writing on the subject of radiesthesia belong to the physicist school as do most other English-speaking writers. The belief of the latter system is that everything has its own vibratory signature and the pendulum enters into resonance with that. To my thinking, it amounts to criminal negligence to ignore the spirit component and focus on the material uniquely, but such is the way of the world.

The probable reason why dowsing has been such a monumental failure in its attempts to break through the barriers erected by the scientific community is, I believe, not only due to an inability to explain where the answer comes from but the lack of credibility caused by the different viewpoints in theory which the various proponents put forward. Let alone the fact that the repetition principle is often at a discount.

Anything that cannot be measured and repeated holds no water for the man of science, even if a solution to the problem is produced to everyone's satisfaction. There is no point arguing with someone who believes life to be solely subject to material scientific principles. What opportunities I have missed because I cannot demonstrate how something works scientifically even if it works empirically! Thank goodness we can opt for a degree of adventure.

Of the French authors, Antoine Luzy stands a head above the rest because of his scope, sincerity and depth of investigation into what he called the psycho-physical aspects of the practice and he broke new ground with his eminently simple approach although rather verbose style of writing, typical of the 1950s. André de Belizal, Léon Chaumery and Pierre Morel, of a purely physicist bent performed interesting research with radionic-type devices and pendulums, taking the show to another level in its unsuspected practical applications and deserve more than a casual study. One of their students, Jean de la Foye, took their work a further step and his book is noteworthy. All of this, however, is in French.

The other side of the English Channel, Aubrey Westlake, Cecil Maby, Guyon Richards have made some useful contributions to the overall scene. Malcolm Rae and David Tansley offered up some interesting ideas to the field of radionics in the steps of Albert Abrams and Ruth Drown. Although Rae and especially Tansley were strongly influenced by theosophy, the fashionable fad of their day with its garbled concepts and perversions.

VITAL FORCE

If we are going to talk of health and life, it might be a good idea initially to find common ground as to a definition of what life is - if such is possible for the life-subscriber.

The invisible but all-pervasive force in living matter is recognized by most humans, and goes by a variety of epithets we are all familiar with, *chi*, *prana*, od, and so on. For the sake of simplicity, it will be Vital Force from here on. Having said that, I would strongly suggest that force is also present in "non-living" matter, hence the latter should also be included in to a larger category, at least for the sake of understanding.

This differentiation between living and non-living is obviously not of my fabrication. It seems to be a widely used concept, like organic and inorganic, sentient and non-sentient; I would insist that such a notion is highly subjective and determined by duration of existence – at which we humans, with our three score years and ten, are not very strong. For example, a rock, for many it is just a lump of stone. For others, especially the radiesthesist, it has a magnetic force, even if it is diamagnetic (very low magnetic charge), therefore alive, in the sense of possessing a force, and by inference, a purpose. Having said that, the rock might well have been around for several millions of years; the notions of sentience and otherwise then become quite relative in that dimension.

It therefore becomes apparent that this Vital Force is made up of a blend of characteristics, which of course we differentiate to the extent of our ability/need to comprehend what is at play, while most of the time completely missing the essential nature of unicity derived from the fact of its very existence, which gives it life in the first instance!

All this 'philosophical' background is necessary if we are to be on the same page.

Despite the efforts made in the last few centuries to encourage us humans to believe that we control Nature, including the falsehood that we can sustain something in a state of permanence, we all share the suspicion that things change and there is not much we can do about it. It seems, therefore, that it would be just to say that the only constant *is* change. I know from where I'm writing in west Cork that the sky and the light is in constant play, constant flux. That situation is the norm, but not so readily perceptible from the enclosed space of a room in a city, especially when subject to multiple sources of invisible and powerful energies that are so concentrated in urban areas, with the unfortunate consequence of numbing the senses.

The idea of good health suffers from a similar delusion of permanence.

Health is a totally subjective affair, inasmuch as we all have our own individual metabolism, our own system of reacting to the 'frequencies' that impact us. Those frequencies come from a whole host of internal and external sources. Given the instable nature of our environment, often saturated with these frequencies, it is nigh on impossible to say, if we are honest, what exactly the cause and effect might be, even if such a causation was possible given the individual nature of the human makeup.

Perhaps that was the initial thinking behind disease.

If we give a name to a condition, rather than to the immensely complex personalized effect, logic would have it that we can streamline a cure. After all, the theory is it that it is the Vital Force which does the healing so as to preserve life by adapting to environmental changes.

Such a belief risks crediting the Vital Force with only one aspect of change, the building up side of its ability. What about the breaking down facet, which ultimately leads to dissolution and death? After all, life is a complete cycle, encompassing change in all its forms; not just the nice bits.

The Vital Force, being the energy form which concerns us humans immediately and intimately, knows no right or wrong, no good or bad; but it does, overall, seem to ensure a harmonious whole. Quite to whose programme or tune, is a mystery, and is of no importance when living the change which, of course, we can only do in the material, physical body.

If we hold to the theory of Vital Force being the principal influence in the presence/absence of life, there is a logical process we can observe when things go wrong. When we, humans, become unwell, we refer to symptoms to guide us to the cause of the problem. So far that is quite logical as symptoms are the manifestation of changes within. And even in the case of physical injury, the symptoms only happen when there is a disruption to the Vital Force.

But why focus on the manifestation and neglect the upset to the Vital Force? But that is exactly what we do, we insist on knowing the mechanism of the issue. That mechanism is, of course, endless and we get lost in the detail and technical aspects, all the while ignoring the possibility of working on the frequency.

Such upsets can occur for a whole host of possible reasons, but without exception these will impact the Vital Force in the human (animal or plant too) one way or another –

infection, inflammation, stress, fatigue, malnutrition, powerful thought, grief, anger, shock and so on. If we are to be sincere in searching for the cause, we could focus on the imbalance, where the solution lies and how to restore harmony. Apart from some obscure intellectual satisfaction, there seems little point in giving a name to a phenomenon, especially if the frequency is affecting the individual in its own manner due to that person's metabolism and mindset, not due to some universal characteristic specific to a contrived word.

Having said that, all that we can reasonably do is to attempt to restore suitable conditions so that the Vital Force can gain the upper hand in its struggle to restore balance and preserve life. It could even be justifiably said that the symptoms are often the products of such a struggle. If the force is unable to regain balance, the person dies.

The idea of a disease named according to symptom(s) is of no importance when the main issue is curing or containing. The focus is on balance, either to adjust the balance and a return to health, or to keep the imbalance within bearable limits, or recognize that is not possible.

The beauty of the pendulum is the ability to discover the state of imbalance, whether it is temporary, chronic, can be remedied, can be contained, and so on.

Let's now develop the most practical aspect of your new-found skill.

Applying the pendulum to people (animals or plants) so that you understand a little more about the social interaction that is underway.

Bearing in mind all that has been said above, and especially your aim with regard to what you are planning to do; for example, character analysis, vital force radiesthesia, Q&A for yourself or others, and so on, it is essential to have a base standard, which sets a landmark or reference point you might navigate by. You probably will and can develop this idea according to your elected work and application.

The origin of the teaching in this next section is obscure, although there does seem to be a thread of sorts to be found in the books of Chaumery and de Belizal, and Enel (Michel Skariatine). I learned to use it from someone I met in Thailand, at the time a Theravadin monk, who in turn had been taught by a German doctor who has survived the battle of Stalingrad.

Thanks to extensive practical experience and research in the form of further questioning, the current system of 'colours' developed, and continues to be tweaked.

COLOURS

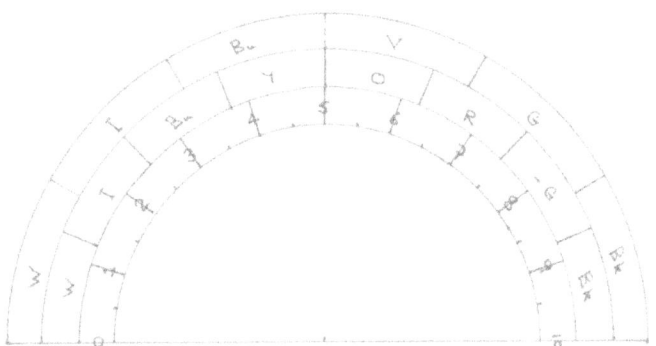

As you can see in the chart above, there are six colours in the top section: W - white, I - indigo, Bu - blue, V - violet, G - green, and Bk - black.
In the intermediate segment, those same colours plus Y - yellow, O - orange, R - red and -G - negative green.

No matter the context - at the start of a dowsing session or out of simple curiosity, you need to know the type of person you are dealing with; nothing could be easier. Take your pendulum and this chart; ask what is this person's external colour, the pendulum will swing towards one of them in the top section.

As explained in my recent publication, *The Way of the Skeptic*:

Colours

Although photons originate in and reach us from the sun, it is only when they reach the earth's atmosphere that they become what we know as light because the vibrational frequencies are transformed to that end by the unique combination of qualities present in the atmosphere, such as pressure and motion. This is but a small part of the story of the many invisible frequencies that impact the earth from the universe; however, the colours are what we are most aware of because they play such an important role in our lives. We are perhaps not so aware that the reason for the specific colours we see are due to the wavelengths of those frequencies, with the colour green, the "colour" of the energy form originating from the sun, having a peak wavelength of 0.45 micrometers. So what we in fact see is a function of the energy form.

A possible parallel could be drawn with astrology, in which the influence of the planets and their electromagnetic and other frequencies makes up a certain component of the human, thanks to the combined terrestrial and cosmic energies at play during the life of the individual. Given that every person has his or her own specific frequential pattern, which can reasonably be assumed to be an aggregate frequency of their cellular vibration, it is but a step to categorize those vibrations into colour.

The origins of these frequencies are multiple, cosmic and telluric, ancestral perhaps, immediate in that they come from the intake of food and drink of the mother, and so on, but they could be regarded as frequencies in seed form of the individual's life purpose, much like an acorn or plant seed. The reason for doing that is purely practical. This aggregate colour in an individual exists, so why not consider it as having a possible correspondence, for example the essence for the person being here. Nothing strange or esoteric should be read into this fact, a person simply has a colour attributed as a function as to how they fulfil their life. This is the colour referred to in the character analysis that I practice. It is an extremely practical function in determining an individual's state of health or otherwise, because this colour must be identical to the individual's internal colour (the sum of all psychosomatic components) for the person to be in balance.

These colours are the conventional seven, red, orange, yellow, green, blue, indigo and violet plus white, black, infrared, ultraviolet, and negative green. Please understand that the use of the word "colour" here in this context involves more than just the optical phenomenon of electromagnetic frequency, for colour can include three distinct phases: electric, magnetic, and electromagnetic.

This broad spectrum was what de Bélizal, Chaumery, and Paul-André Morel were working on, and they found that a number of objects, both natural and manufactured—trees, certain buildings of special geometric architecture, spherical objects—contain the full spectrum of twelve colours. Having found that a half-sphere generates this spectrum, they experimented and soon found that a collection of identical half-spheres set up in series and arranged in a sphere can both project and detect the frequency of the "colour" in question when positioned on a specific axis and equator.

They discovered all this from experimenting with a scale model of the Pyramid of Cheops.

In the same way that what we see with our eyes is a very limited portion of what is actually there because our eyes act as a filter for the brain, providing sufficient information for the immediate need only, likewise perhaps everything we gather through our many antenna senses has this same capacity to conceal an immensity of potentiality that is unknowingly tapped into but ignored except for the immediate necessity. It would make sense that this "mechanism" is one of survival, and what a masterpiece. But what does it imply for the larger picture of existence and its way of operation—the domain of knowledge?

The hypothesis here is that an individual's "external physical colour" is a frequential manifestation. I would hasten to add that this has no relation to the "aura" mentioned above as revealed by Dr. Walter Kilner, which, when applied by him, is an indication of the individual's organic condition along the lines of thermography.

All external colours referred to here are in the electric phase, probably because such a current originates from the heart's electrical impulse, and what I refer to as the "internal" colour, is of a magnetic nature.

The colour generally does not change during the life of an individual but can still be detected from a photograph of a person or from his or her name and date of birth, an item of clothing, or some other item even after physical death. Under some circumstances, the colour can change during a person's lifetime, but that will be discussed at a later stage.

Obviously, humans are not the only beings that share this colour-frequency manifestation. Everything does, which is what the physicist school of dowsing picks up on. Water also contains this frequency, in the electric phase too, but it is more an indication of the water's maturity, therefore quality.

These colours are in close relation to the human makeup, an impression of their aggregate quality but not to be confused with the emotional, spiritual, mental, and physical states, which can be determined with reference to the internal colour, as such components are subject to constant change as experienced in the ups and downs of life.

Individual people are associated with one of six colours, which, as mentioned earlier, generally stays with the person his or her entire life. A number of useful indications can be gleaned from these colours, which are:

- *white,*
- *violet,*
- *indigo,*
- *blue,*
- *green, and*
- *black.*

Enel (Michel V. Skariatine), a Russian radiesthesist who worked in the medical dowsing field, employing a similar method, recognizes only four colours, stating that green is not found among humans; he makes no mention of black.

External Colours

It is now time to tread warily, for we are on thin ice, being in the domain where nothing can be scientifically posited but everyday experience confirms the consensus sentiment. Fortunately, the pendulum is here to confirm that what is said is the truth.

The main characteristics of these colours are as follows:

- ***White*** *is a manifestation of harmony; "white" people are few and far between. The individual becomes white as a result of effort; I believe that people are not born with this colour.*

- ***Violet*** *people often have a mission in their life, and nothing will get in their way in the quest to accomplish that objective. Some famous examples include Mahatma Gandhi, Mother Teresa, Joseph Stalin, Adolf Hitler, Pol Pot, Cecil Rhodes, and Mao Zedong. Very often, if not systematically, violet people are not alone in their "life" space, possessed as they are by an intention that is not of their own device. This violet colour changes once the "personality" is cleared.*

- ***Indigo*** *seemingly indicates people who are more spiritually rather than materialistically oriented. It is one of the two colours found among "normal" people, those who labour as best they can, doing what they believe is in the best interests of one and all. The hun are in predominance in indigo people's behaviour, and although the po are active, they do not generally get out of hand resulting in excess.*

- ***Blue*** *is a commonly found colour. Blue people are much in keeping with indigo but with the difference that the po are inclined to gain the upper hand, and behaviour is more earth-oriented. These people are more readily subject to excess than indigo persons, but with their heart in the right place with regard to others.*

- ***Green*** *is very rare in humans; I have only ever found it in one individual, whose brain was severely impaired as the result of a motorbike accident.*

- ***Black*** *is the colour of persons dominated by the po, the hun having most probably fled. This is not a good condition to be in; it is very unhealthy for persons hosting the colour as well as for those in their presence, although the former are unlikely to notice, let alone be bothered. People imposing their will on others due to overwhelming egoism are often of this colour. To avoid being* *sued for defamation, I will name no examples, but they are numerous and found in all walks of life; black people are increasingly common. This is an acquired colour; people are not born in this condition but deliberately opt for it. The predominant emotion manifested by such people is hate in one form or another.*

Animals and plants, without exception, do not share this colour scheme in its diversity; they are all green, systematically.

The purpose of this colour scheme is primarily for analysis; it is not a score sheet intended to judge people, so be careful of reading too much into its interpretation, although it is very useful to know what kind of person one is dealing with. The analysis is based on the balance (or imbalance) of external and internal colours; if they are the same, all well and good, but if not, there is imbalance, and further investigation is necessary to find where the problem, if any, lies. This system is a remarkable way to help establish harmony in individual existence.

As concerns the balance or imbalance between internal and external colour, more is to follow after we have taken a closer look at the 'black' people.

Without overly dramatizing, I think it is perfectly justified to state that human egocentricity has bloomed in recent centuries, particularly in western cultures where ever since the Reformation, the governing structure of society has been eroded. This is merely to say that due to the western lack of morality, compared to the Hindu or Confucian ethic, it has been progressively easier for people to get away with things that would not have been accepted by the majority a few centuries ago. When one combines this removal of restraint with the irresponsibility we entertain with regard to our well-being and employment, it is scarcely surprising that it is every man for himself, and increasingly so everywhere irrespective of societal or religious ethic.

Energy apparently knows neither right, nor wrong. It is a force that works on king and pauper alike. We access that force quite readily in our everyday activities, by thinking, by breathing, by metabolizing what we eat and drink, by sleeping, and so on. Quite with what consequences is another matter, but in some form or another we all, human, animal or plant, participate in sharing this life force. Is it stretching the imagination too far to believe that the aggregated energy force can be focussed and channelled to good or bad, god or devil?

Is it not what we do when forming a desire? You work, materially or psychologically, towards an objective in order to achieve it. If we were materially unable to accomplish our wants, we would probably have given up on desires a long time ago.

The thin line between what is good or bad seems to depend on the quantity of people who benefit, as opposed to the number who find themselves at a disadvantage. Obviously, the individual knows whether their action is altruistic or egocentric. It could reasonably be said that everything we humans do, is egocentric. And this is where the idea of a scale comes in. From 0 to 10, zero being weak, 10 being strong. In the same way, how black is a person? As a rule of thumb, I consider a score of 6 as the cut-off point, anything above that, it is best to steer clear of the individual. Below that median, they are still determined to get their way, but will hopefully stop short when shown that there is resistance sufficient to curtail or hamper their schemes.

In an attempt to define this scale of 'blackness':
1. Ego and what I want
2. Ego first and foremost
3. Manipulation without compunction
4. Sophisticated veneer concealing rather sordid characteristics
5. Perversity
6. Bandit, loose cannon
7. Black arts in progress – danger
8. To be avoided, highly dangerous
9. To be avoided, highly dangerous and not confronted
10. Evolved black arts, to be avoided, highly dangerous and not confronted

There is a common thread to history which is rarely, if ever, pointed out. The sequel of events that forms history, as recorded by humans, is most often determined by the actions/desires of an individual. The results, of the events that get into the history books, are far-reaching for humanity and Nature. Yet, the majority of characters that made the history books are either black or violet in external colour.

What is rather vaguely referred to as black magic could be considered as the excessive use of the life force in a single-minded effort to achieve one's personal objectives. When practiced in ritual form, it is seemingly reinforced with the years of intention built-up behind the scenes, and it becomes very convincing. In my practice, this kind of magic often raises its head and is cause for a lot of head-scratching, rethinking and stress.

While there seem to be a number of counter-acting measures, the solution invariably needs to be found via the notion that 'all is one', so rather than confront the force – obligatorily stronger than yourself – which thrives on fear and hate, one has every interest to find common ground, that can only lie in the domain of energy and its manifestation of desire. That common ground, I believe, is concealed in the craving (a warped form of love) of the magician, and the minions he/she employs (they are in this worldly domain having failed, for one reason or another, to move to the unity of existence at the time of their physical death).

Clearly, one does not go and knock on the magician's door to suggest a parlay. So, one has to deal with the daunting energy forms, or entities, as best one can. Without going into the multifarious complications that such encounters involve – and every time is different – the aim is to come to grips/terms, and adopting a page from the Kahuna tradition, convince the beast to change its spots, or something along those lines!

Once again, falling back on time-tested practices, such a relationship can only be lastingly accomplished in love, compassion and empathy. The final objective being the release of the 'entity' from its bondage. Naturally, that implies that the magician loses a valued ally. That will not happen without some resistance, and a war of attrition is not unusual. On one side, the gradual weakening of the 'dark' forces as new recruits – indeed, that is what they are, errant spirits entering the service in exchange for some form of reward; and, on the other, a clearing up in the life of the oppressed client as balance and weal are slowly restored. As in any war, there are many battles, reverses, ambushes and upset of plans.

This might well be a major delusion on my part, or a metaphorical allegory. No matter what or how one interprets events, at the end of the day, there is only one criterion to be heeded – harmony.

Everything in Nature strives for harmony, and we are no different.

SPIRIT RELEASE

While we are on the subject of delusion, I think spirit release, or aiding disembodied entities to find the way to the light of Consciousness accounts for the majority of my activity. The reason for that is perhaps to be found in the rather strange fact that 60% (a conservative estimate) of people have what one might call "spirit attachments". What on earth makes me think it is possible for another human to help another form of being? I hear screams of protest, and, rest assured I often doubt my sanity, veracity, and other supposed human characteristics.

Some years ago, when tackling a very heavy and terrifying entity whom I was attempting to befriend in the hope of getting the fiend to lay off a client who had asked me for help in finding some relief, I had the opportunity to ask some questions of the 'personality'. The answers were very graciously provided, including the intriguing information that a pendulum of a specific form – the Karnak – when generating by its geometric design what de Belizal and Chaumery baptized "negative green in the electric phase", could act as a frequency on which to travel. Not for you and I, however, at least not yet. This frequency appears to establish a link for the disembodied entity here in this worldly dimension to integrate the light of Consciousness, and so leave the physical dimension definitively.

It appears to be the right tool for me. There are surely other means to achieve that objective, and as always, the pendulum is there to help find the solution.

I am neither a spiritist nor spiritualist, but reading Allan Kardec (Hipolyte Rivail), Carl Wickland, Oliver Lodge and other classics in that genre proved to be useful to formulate a *modus operandi* in what risks becoming a career if you open your mind to this path of working with the invisible.

As with so many theories put forward out there, one has every interest in thinking through the forest and taking what is opportune and practically useful, and leave the rest. The truth of today might well change tomorrow, and the resulting confusion is only painful if you tend towards reactionarism – being rigid and conservative, refusing change.

Dealing with the spirit world is not to every one's liking and there is absolutely no obligation to get involved in it just because you swing a pendulum. The subject is raised because it is very much there, and is very REAL, and a regular part of my activity.

Before returning to more familiar territory, mention could well be made of some tricks of the trade, so to speak. You will find your own ways and means as your practice develops, but the experience of others is not to be spurned.

Mention has already been made above of using an object (a pet rock has my favour) held in the hand so as to divert one's focus away from the question asked. Putting the 'yes' and 'no' cards in an envelope too, as explained in Radiesthesia I.

In the world of smoke and mirrors of magic, the answers to questions posed with the pendulum are almost invariably inversed. This can be disconcerting, but to be expected; you are being a nuisance in the plans of people who are used to being obeyed. The field of influence – whatever nature that assumes – is extensive and there is a good chance you are within it.

THE THUMBKEY

A *mudra*, or position of the fingers of the hand not holding the pendulum, has the capacity to offset the 'magic' miasma. Bring the tip of your little finger ("pinkey") into contact with the tip of your thumb, and ask the question again.

In Charles Kreb's Learning Enhancement Acupressure Program, this type of *mudra* is standard and constant practice.

This simple gesture works well, and the image of the surprise on the face of a **BIDORT**-practitioner friend some years ago is still with me. I had asked him to check the strength of the Thumbkey compared with the regular hand position. It has surprising qualities.

FACTORS IN ANALYSIS

No matter the eventual application when you use the pendulum for analyzing the balance or otherwise of a person, there are a number of factors that are indicative of the individual's state of being which are best to check. If you find others, as you will doubtless do in accordance with your practice and applications, please consider sharing them with me.

Analysis can be accomplished in person or remotely. The procedure for both follows much the same lines. The advantage of physical presence is the possibility of asking for confirmation and seeing/feeling the reactions. There are occasions when remote-work is easier because neutrality is more natural.

The scoring system is based on a scale of zero to ten, with fractions if you like. Zero is the lowest point, with ten at the opposite end. By and large, it would seem that 6.5 is the cutoff point between reasonable and problematic, but that is very much for each practitioner to establish, obviously in the specific context.

WITNESS

If you work remotely, you will need what is referred to as a 'witness'. The old school radiesthesists worked on sputum, a blood sample or a lock of hair. Modernity would have us believe that such like are health hazards, let alone the dangers involved in taking your own blood out of a finger, or cutting a curl! Not to worry, a photo of the client – alone – even an old one, OR their name and date of birth are quite sufficient.

That does eliminate the chance of a joker sending you a cutting from the dog's coat. There is further the possibility of the photo of someone deceased. Checking their electric current will determine that; it drops to 0 at death.

Write the name and date of birth of the person to be analyzed on a piece of card paper, perhaps 5 x 5 cm. It is not a bad idea to have a filing system if you are going to work on the person regularly, so as to keep things tidy and have a record to follow progress – or the reverse.

DIAGNOSIS/ANALYSIS

An assessment sheet is provided at the end of this text as inspiration. Having established who and the date, inscribe the person's name, gender, date of birth, time and place (for possible astrological insights); the next question concerns the colour (external) of the individual. As expressed above, this potentially indicates a number of things, foremost of which is if the colour is violet. That is not their 'true' colour, inasmuch as once the imposing entity/hitch-hiker has gone/has been released, the person's colour will change.

Should the colour be violet, ask how many entities/fragments/spirits? Quite what the nature of these influences are is as diverse as the human dimension. So, in the interest of not losing oneself in the possibilities, although it is always a good idea to remain open to unforeseen eventualities, keep it simple, within your reasoning ability and the person's explanation. Remember that 'possession' can be a voluntary choice on the part of the individual, or involuntary, as in the case of possession by curse. You may usefully enquire of the origin of these invaders, it often helps in their release, especially if it is a family member who did not want to exit at the opportune moment. But we will look into this more in detail elsewhere.

Then the internal colour is to be verified, again referring to the Way of the Skeptic:

Internal Colours

Having determined the person's external colour, one then asks what the internal colour is. If identical to the external, all well and good, but if not, there is imbalance. The internal colours number nine: white, violet, indigo, blue, yellow, orange, red, black, and negative green. As mentioned above, if the individual is violet, the first thing to do is to clarify and, if possible, resolve the situation by releasing the personality/ties. In any case, it is always a good idea to check if there is interference on a psychic level, for very often the root of a problem can be attributed to an invasive presence, but more on that later.

The yellow colour is generally due to an organic issue affecting the liver, the seat of the hun. Orange most often is caused by poison, alimentary intoxication, or some other externally caused problem such as from an insect bite or sting, even the mother-in-law. *Red indicates emotion or extreme fatigue. Black is a danger sign indicating a critical situation on the cusp, which can either revert back to harmony or flip to negative green, which is very critical.*

....

Chinese feng shui practitioners use a tool called a bagua (pakua), a circular device with a basis of eight trigrams, to analyze energy and its manifestation; it also has a colour scheme corresponding to the trigrams, but that is another kettle of fish.

This brings us to a question which will [perhaps] never be unanimously resolved.

Is there not something immaterial that remains after the physical death of the body?

The magnetic component

The next step in the diagnosis concerns just this 'something immaterial', the magnetic or biomagnetic field of the person, this is an immensely useful indicator of human well-being and ranges in measurement from 15 to 75; there is no unit of measurement *per se* and no registering of the electron spin or other movement. The unit of measurement used to record the magnetic field of the earth is a microtesla, ranging between 25 and 65 microteslas for the earth's charge, I suspect that this same value can be applied to this human factor. Quite what this expression of movement is can be explained in a variety of ways, but I don't think that really helps our understanding. It is probably a function of the life energy, the Chinese *qi* or the Vedic *prana*. The strength of such an element in a living human varies according to many factors: exposure to electromagnetic radiation, the strength or otherwise of the immune system, the wearing of shoes, environmental influences, physical sickness, emotional well-being, and so on.

It can be boosted, and that is very good news because our entire environment is gradually being weakened magnetically.

It is useful to know the magnetic polarity of the person's hands, because if you are working on them in person, it is best to work on the positively charged hand. Generally speaking, men have a positive charge emanating from the palm of their right hand and a negative one from the left. Men who were born prematurely or who are gay often have an inverse polarity, making the left palm the positive and the right, negative.

Women, in contrast, have a positive charge emanating from the palm of their *left* hand; women born prematurely or who are lesbian may have inverse polarity, and almost invariably at menopause their polarity switches, the right hand becoming positive and the left negative. This last observation might explain the severe changes to women's hormonal system, as experienced with flashes and other uncomfortable effects. It is not an instantaneous reversal but a gradual process, hence the inconvenience and discomfort of menopause lasting in some cases for several years. The condition of being right- or left-handed, even ambidextrous, seems to make little or no difference to the biomagnetic polarity of the palm of the hand.

The images below shows the locations of general biomagnetic points in the human body as explained above.

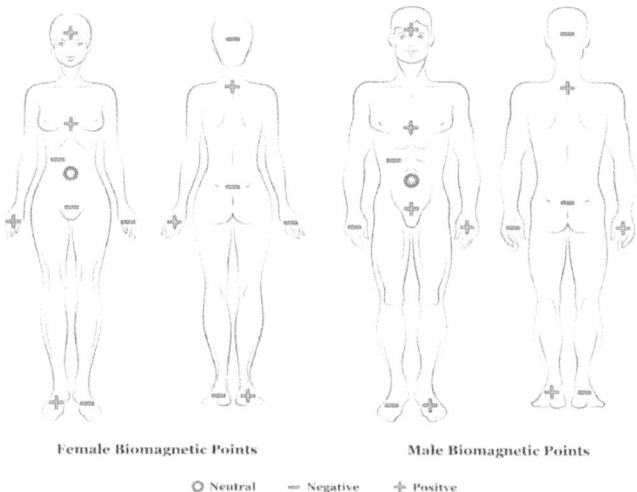

Female Biomagnetic Points   Male Biomagnetic Points

O Neutral   — Negative   + Positve

Another constant in human biomagnetism resides in the spine and head and this applies to man and woman alike. Systematically, the front of the head (forehead) is positive, which is probably due to the energetic flow of the telluric force streaming outward at the level of the eyes via the pineal gland, and the cosmic frequencies coming in through the top of the head to access the pituitary gland before spreading down through the body. The back of the head is negative.

With the same constancy, the back of the hand will have the opposite polarity to the palm, irrespective of the polarity of the palm. If the left hand is positive, the right foot will be positive too, and vice versa for the right hand and left foot. The top of the spine is systematically positive and the base of the spine negative, useful for the positioning of biocircuits in relation to the hands and feet.

The naturally harmonious, positive and negative arrangement of biomagnetic polarity in the human body is generally constant for the duration of a lifetime. There are circumstances in which certain aspects of the arrangement can change, most notably for women at menopause, when their biomagnetic polarity changes. This fact is patently ignored by modern medicine, perhaps most other systems too; however, there is some relief to be found in magnetic recharging.

Of the vital organs, only two have a constant polarity throughout the lifetime of the individual, and these are the heart with a positive polarity, and the liver with negative. It is of interest to record the magnetic and electric reading score for the liver and heart, this will give a better indication of the state of the functioning of these organs. The readings are generally different from the overall 'magnetic' and 'electric' readings.

The reason for that would appear to be that the flow of blood and nervous energy in the body are the main forces creating the electric current, and the magnetic field will be in proportion to the electric current, on condition that there are no other blockages/leaks potentially causing loss of field.

The magnetic recharging posture allows you to recharge your biomagnetic field in just a few minutes. Regardless of the polarity in the hands, interlace your fingers, and let your hands rest on your stomach or chest. The polarities will be joined, negative and positive. Now, your feet. Those with right-handed positive polarity, put your left foot over the right ankle. Conversely, for left-handed positive polarity, put the right foot over the left ankle. You will find out after five minutes if you made the wrong choice. You will feel enervated, so change the position of your feet.

With hands and feet joined, sitting at your desk, on the bus, lying down, wherever, you have closed the biomagnetic loop of the body's field and are recharging. Why do that? As explained above, the current of the blood's movement through the veins and the energy through the meridians result in an electric charge, which can be measured in millivolts. Ten millivolts, and you are at death's door; at seventy millivolts—and you will not get higher—you are fighting fit. Most people come in at twenty-five millivolts, which is weak, further indicating that the immune system is probably struggling.

No one, to my knowledge, has ever pointed out that this is just what you are doing when sitting cross-legged in meditation, one hand in the other, but no matter. One often sees old people in this position; maybe their bodies react instinctively.

Contrary to what many people maintain, the polarity of human limbs can change, but that may be a recent phenomenon due to the surge in the past one hundred or so years of electricity, mobile telephony, wireless devices, personal computers and other electronic gear, air travel, the earth's weakening magnetic field (due to the extraction of oil and minerals), and so forth, likely resulting in the perturbed magnetic patterns commonly encountered nowadays.

TW2 – PRESENCE OF GEOPATHIC STRESS (GS)

The Triple Warmer (San Jiao) meridian runs from the tip of the ring finger, up the arm, over the shoulder, around the ear, to the eyebrow. The number 2 point, or the 'Door of the Humours', used in acupuncture or moxibustion to stimulate the *shen*, indicates if the person is sleeping or living over geopathic stress. You just need to dangle a pendulum over this point on their positive magnetic hand, at the joint of the annular and middle fingers, and if the swing is negative, you know there is a problem of telluric energy at home or in the work-place.

There is every reason to believe that the first thing to do on discovering the presence of GS, is to remove it. For the simple reason, a person who exists in that condition, cannot get better so long as they stay there. On the contrary, there is every chance health will deteriorate. This factor cannot be stressed enough.

RESISTANCE

This is a delicate matter, and probably best not to reveal the finding to the person. Many people are content in their suffering. That may appear to be a strange, even horrible thing to say. But believe me it is far worse for the family members living with such individuals, while probably not being very gay for those in that frame of existence. Without informing the client what you are asking; ask if the person really wants to get better, if the answer is no, ask on a scale of 0-10, what is their resistance to recovering. Up to you what you then decide to do, personally I let the client slowly drop away if that score is over 6/10. You cannot fight someone else's battle for them, even if you might be able to offer guidance.

Malcom Rae added further questions, such as: resistance against being cured of disease; resistance against being healthy. That is most probably best to be developed on an individual basis as a function of the conscious or otherwise belief in the need for the imbalance or disease as found in the person. All this is the backdrop for reasons preventing, delaying, limiting and rendering only temporary, the curing of imbalance and the restoration and maintenance of good health. Up to you to determine how far one needs to discover these facts, for they may or not be useful factors in the process.

GENERAL STATE

This is the overall bellwether indicator. As a function of the person's age, if the reading is over 9, there is a strong chance that there is no need for you. The score indicates an aggregate of the following component states. It might be worth checking which of the following factors is bringing the overall score down, so as to address the issue in a more coherent fashion.

EMOTIONAL STATE

The majority of people in my experience come in with the colour red. It might be a temporary issue or a chronic one, always ask and record the answer. If the person's internal colour indicates red, there is either an emotional issue, or extreme fatigue, sometimes a combination of both those.

Generally speaking, that issue is covered by the seven emotional categories enumerated by the Chinese, namely: fear, anger, sadness, excitement, worry, overthinking (melancholia) and shock. Quite often, people don't recognize the problem in such a neat category, so some flexibility in interpretation might be needed. For the Chinese, an emotional upset was a sign that an organ was out of balance. While that may be an over-simplification, it is much easier to work on those lines rather than some psychological mumbo-jumbo. Having the seven emotions on a chart is a practical start but you might need to expand that list; I have one with sixty-four but it is not as handy!

It is very important to remember that all you can hope to do is help others organize their emotions. But the simple fact of pointing out that an organ is impacted by an emotional condition can be revealing to the person in question and become a turning point for behavior.

NERVOUS STATE

In the interest of narrowing down the origins of a problem, it is useful to have a score for the nervous condition. From this score you can trace the evolution of the factors forming its composition. Stress is the cause of so many issues and it can be a good idea to pinpoint the culprit. Very often the emotional, mental and nervous state merge and it is tricky to locate the exact components, but it is a great help to investigate further if the score is low. Breathing is an essential influence on a harmonious nervous system, always best to verify a person's breathing function if they are in front of you. Work, home, GS, family, relationships, sleep, EMR could be usefully queried with a view to suggesting ideas or recommendations of an alternative nature.

MENTAL STATE

A score to this category indicates the strength of 'mind'. The state of flux, agitation of the person's mental activity, the force or weakness of mental capacity, are in turn due to all sorts of factors, which may be useful to discover so that the person can expand on them to find solutions if needed. Often in cases of exhaustion, one finds that the person is keeping it all 'together' thanks to their strength of mind. That can be cause for a very critical condition, as cracks can appear. This is where discovering the real nature of such a situation in time can provide a useful signal to rest, or at least change tack, if danger is to be avoided.

VITAL FORCE

This is an indication of the strength or otherwise of the individual's vital force, or whatever one prefers to call the life energy that flows through a metabolism. Further questioning along the lines as to why this indicator is weak produces information that can contribute to a better picture of the person's state, especially if it is at the onset of a problem.

In all the above five categories, one can usefully ask, rather than just a score, a number of additional questions that can add considerable light to the situation. For example, what is the optimal score for the individual in question; is it a temporary, chronic or terminal phase; the time scale of that phase; whether an improvement or the opposite is to be expected, and by what bias or therapeutic system.

HUN AND PO

This is a specifically Chinese concept which is developed succinctly in *The Way of the Skeptic*. These two play a major role in the context of psychic balance, and that is why they are found here. If there are three *hun* and seven *po* present in the person, all well and good. If there is one or more missing the roll-call, ask if they are still close by and if they can reintegrate. Outside help might be needed in such cases.

MAGNETISM

The stronger the magnetic reading is, the better. It will not go beyond 75 and cannot drop below 15. As mentioned above, even when a person is dead the magnetic component will register 15. The majority of people come in with 20-25, that is too weak and the magnetic recharging exercise would be a good idea, as well as better quality water, grounding perhaps, and definitely less EMR.

ELECTRIC CURRENT

Caused by the flow of blood and nervous energy, a very indicative sign of the state of the immune system. At death the heart stops and the current stands at 0. The closer one can get to the maximum of 70, the better. The measurement is in millivolts and is similar to the range found in electrocardiograms, etc.

There now follows a series of factors that play a potentially significant role in the balance of well-being. The first two, EMR and nuclear radiation, are unavoidable in today's world.

ELECTROMAGNETIC RADIATION (EMR)

There is probably little point in measuring this unless you have the means to reduce the radiation. An orgone accumulator (OA) can do that, although frequent visits – twenty minutes every three weeks or so – are required, perhaps more often in case of 5G. It does enable an awareness, however, of the downside of our favourite toys – internet, laptops, phones, etc. Electro-sensitivity is an increasingly common condition, and an extremely painful one it is too. There are few doctors who recognize it as such and it is often relegated to a psychological ill.

NUCLEAR RADIATION

Much the same applies here, to my knowledge the only solution for nuclear radiation is the OA. Iodine and seaweed are severely compromised by the prevalent radiation levels in the oceans throughout the world. It is fundamentally impossible to have a base reading from a Geiger counter, for the simple reason a counter can no longer be calibrated outside of a clean room.

A great many thyroid problems find their origin in nuclear radiation pollution, which has been going on for decades now, but much exacerbated by the Fukushima "China syndrome". The Orgone Accumulator is a life-saver in this context.

INFECTION

Indicates the presence or not of an infection. Have space on the chart for a virus and/or bacteria option. Referring to the 12 Chinese organs, one can usefully ask for the locality of the infection and its degree of severity.

Increasingly today, the flora of the small intestine appears to be the culprit, especially candida and geotrichum. While there may be immediate solutions for bacteria, such as *e.coli*, with turpentine, the remedies for fungal issues can be usefully sought for in phago- and hemo-therapy, fortunately still practised in some eastern European countries.

INFLAMMATION

Presence and location of inflammation, as with infection. Diet and water can frequently provide relief, so worth asking such questions.

POISON

Often when the internal colour is orange, the cause is poison. One needs to ask if this is internal or external, and then track it down. Something ingested, habitual or exceptional. Is it from water, nutrition, environment, psychic, mental, physical, emotional, telluric, cosmic, or other. This type of issue can range from allergies to the mother-in-law to toothpaste, so get your thinking cap on.

NUTRITION

The most time-consuming aspect is when one discovers that a person's imbalance is caused by nutrition. Only go down that path if they are totally committed to changing diet, and probably their life-style. One has to work through a long list of products and combinations. It is sometimes easier to ask what is the most harmful, if there is a need to remove that completely from the diet. Once again, think through the context and allow intuition to guide you.

LIFE-STYLE

Another of those categories where discretion is called upon. There is no point suggesting someone stops smoking, drinking alcohol, abusing substances unless they want to do so. The only thing to do is to point out that the person is harming themselves.

WATER

The importance of water cannot be emphasized sufficiently, to my mind. Not just the quantity but the quality. Ask what is the right quantity for the person to drink in general; then ask if their quality of water is correct. If the quality is dubious, try to find a better water – by asking what is available, preferably in a glass bottle. BPA and phthalates are bad news.

Do not hesitate asking if the water a person is using has an adequate pH. There is a good chance that the higher the alkalinity of water consumed, the less acidity will be generated, and perhaps even the possibility of reducing the level in the system. So, check and see.

CLIMATE

Climate-sensitivity is often a factor of imbalance, chronic or seasonal. Make a reading of the score from 0-10 so as to monitor evolution. There is a link between the magnetic field and this form of sensitivity, which may provide a key to a solution.

The following factors would also be well to check: Development issues, Hospitalization, Vaccination, Metals, Allergies, Medication, Parasites. Questioning with the pendulum can be most useful in these matters, but beware of the controversial position that can easily arise if the person is inclined towards conventional, allopathic medicine.

A key to any such analysis is compassion, there is no point telling a person that they need to change climate if they cannot envisage such a possibility. Solutions need to be found in the accessible, and they often can be found if there is a will and imagination.

ORIGIN

If a chronic problem is found, there is some considerable interest in determining what the origin is. The following categories might provide a lead to a possible solution:
Water – Nutrition – Environment – Psychic – Mental – Physical – Emotional – Telluric – Cosmic – Other.

TEMPERAMENT

The traditional four temperaments of astrology, or those developed by Galen are frequently a source or indication that can be usefully determined, especially in character analysis: Choleric – Sanguine – Melancholic – Phlegmatic.

BIO-CHEMISTRY

Working along the lines of JER McDonagh's theory concerning the protein cycle in the human metabolism, it is of interest to discover potentially at what stage the process might be disrupted: Attraction – Storage – Radiating;
and where: Pineal – Supracortex – Ante-Pituitary – Parathyroid – Thymus – Islets of Langerhaans – Thyroid – Chromaffin – Post-Pituitary – Gonad/Ovary.

pH, rH_2 and ro of Blood and Urine

Working along the lines of Louis-Claude Vincent's theory, as developed in Bioelectronics, it can be very instructive to learn more about a person's blood and urine. This is done via the pH score. As a function of the results, suggest requesting further testing to verify the findings. Not just a reading for the pH of blood and urine, but rH_2, the degree of concentration in electrons, (scale of 0-42) indicates possible build-up of free radicals. The viscosity or resistivity factor, ro, indicates the concentration of electrolytes (molecules, ions or mineral salts).
Very often a water dynamized by gold, silver or other metal can provide not only relief, but a remedy.

DIGESTION

One of the most pertinent, because an area of increasing and widespread problems, it is most useful to learn of a person's **appetite** and/or **eating disorders**, especially **bowel movement** and its nature. Any **aversions, cravings, addiction** can be indicative of the individual's state of being and where the issue lies.

BREATHING

It is surprising the number of people who need to be reminded of how important it is to breathe. There are numerous breathing techniques aiding so many different conditions, but so many people who ignore the most basic rule of health – physical, mental, nervous and emotional.

ORGANS

Using the 0-10 scale, it is most practical to record a score for each of the TCM organs. It is also useful to establish an hierarchical order to determine an order of emphasis for attention. In chronological order: **Gall Bladder** (11pm-1am), **Liver** (1-3am), **Lung** (3-5am), **Large Intestine** (5-7am), **Stomach** (7-9am), **Spleen** (9-11am), **Heart** (11am-1pm), **Small Intestine** (1-3pm), **Urinary Bladder** (3-5pm), **Kidneys** (5-7pm), **Pericardium** (7-9pm), **Triple Warmer** (9-11pm).

ENDOCRINE SYSTEM

As above, record the score for each of the endocrines: Pineal, Pituitary, Parathyroid, Thyroid, Thymus, Pancreas, Adrenal, Ovary, Testes.

END

Assessment Sheet

Date:

Name: DOB:
Time: Place: Gender:
Polarity RH   LH   Ext colour: Int colour:
Nervous tension: TW2:   Poss. vol/invol: Resistance:
General state: Emotional: Nervous:
Mental: Vital force: Hun: Po:
Magnetism: Elect curr: EMR: Nuclear:

Infection: Inflammation: Poison:
Nutrition: Life-style: Water qnty/qlty:
Weather: Development issue: Hospitalization:
Vaccine: Metals: Allergies:
Medication: Parasites:
Origin of problem: Water Nutrition Environment
Psychic Mental Physical Emotional Telluric Cosmic Other
Choleric: Sanguine: Melancholic: Phlegmatic:
Attraction: Storing: Radiating:
Pineal Supracortex Ante-Pituitary Parathyroid
Thymus Islets of Langerhaans Thyroid Chromaffin
Post-Pituitary Gonad/Ovary
pH : Blood Urine
rH_2 : Blood Urine
ro : Blood Urine
Appetite: Eating disorders: Digestion:
Bowel movement: Breathing: Aversions:
Craving: Addiction: Sleep: Dreaming:
Lv H Lu SI Sp St Ki
LI P TW GB UB Du Ren
Pineal ParaThy Thymus Adrenal
Pituitary Thyroid Pancreas Ovary/Testes
Major concerns Other
Recommend Misc:

About the author

The basis of this text is founded essentially on a combination of practical experience, the study of theory from books, substantial personal practice and experimentation in a variety of methods and traditions. It all started in India in the early seventies when I studied Sanskrit so as to read the ancient texts in the original rather than relying on translation. In that phase, I had the opportunity to study with Swami Pranav Tirtha, a *dashnami sannyasin*, who initiated me into the Vedanta philosophy. Whilst with him I read, studied and assimilated the orthodox teachings of the Upanisads, the Brahma Sutra, Gita and multiple metaphysical and sundry texts of Hindu literature. I was ordained as a monk, with the name of Swami Chidananda Tirtha in May 1973. This period also furnished the occasion to study medicine with Dr Himatlal Trivedi, an Ayurvedic practitioner from Palitana, whom I accompanied in India and Africa in his practice amongst English and Gujerati-speaking patients. That involved study of the Hindu medical classics (Caraka Samhita, Sushruta Samhita, Ashtanga Hrdaya), with considerable practical experimentation of fasting and dietary regime on myself. Observation with Himatlal's guidance and explanation gave me a reasonable understanding of this medical art form.

Whilst living in France, I had the opportunity to study for a year with a French acupuncturist, who was persuaded to come out of retirement to teach Traditional Chinese Medicine (TCM) again. That grounding was then followed by many years of studying the Chinese classics: the Lingshu, the Huainanzi, the Suwen, along with in-depth reading of Soulié de Morant, Claude Larre and Elisabeth Rochat de la Vallée, in addition to extensive practice of moxibustion and acupressure. Whilst living in Chiang Mai, the opportunity arose to learn and practice a form of bio-energetics which involved a lot of practical moxibustion. The outcome of my studies of TCM affords a certain ease with this very complete approach to the human condition.

A vast amount of research, reading and experimentation with a very broad spectrum of subjects, traditions and cultures, combined with travelling and living among natives of other lands, along with my professional activity as a technical translator, specialized in nuclear and telecom technologies, for some twenty-five years in France have hopefully been turned to good advantage.

Study, practice and research into magnetism, laying on of hands, geomancy, radiesthesia and radionics add to my wholistic comprehension of life. A practice of organic farming combined with animal husbandry, special care for water and its supply have also lead to my current understanding. I work more with the intention of clarifying what I think seems to be happening in the dimensions we evolve in, rather than any kind of dogmatic laying down of law.

Whilst I sincerely believe my opinions to be correct because corroborated by the pendulum and experience, it would be a substantial error to think this is the last word because it concerns uniquely what falls within my own sensory (all three hundred and sixty) parameters. Too much is changing too fast for our perceptual ability to stay abreast of events, even were we able to comprehend and adapt. Perhaps it is not for us humans to determine how the ordered immensity of Nature works; that would be most presumptuous and dishonest; but it does seem to be worth trying to establish a mode of operation that might serve as a guide or possible reference fitting into our journey through this phenomenal existence.

I stand on the shoulders, hopefully in rectitude and fidelity to the thrust of the original argument of many researchers, practitioners and remarkable people in aligning these words on paper. The words will, as always, be symbols of the generosity of Nature as she carefully keeps everything in its structured place, although the human component must be the most unruly, hence the hard lessons we have to learn if we aspire to some other form of existence than the purely material.

www.ingramcontent.com/pod-product-compliance
Lightning Source LLC
Chambersburg PA
CBHW081422080526
44589CB00016B/2644